ACTIVE SCIENCE

Magnets

This edition 2004

First published in 1994 by
Franklin Watts
96 Leonard Street
London EC2A 4XD

Franklin Watts Australia
45-51 Huntley Street
Alexandria NSW 2015

Copyright © 1994 Franklin Watts

Editorial planning: Serpentine Editorial
Scientific consultant: Dr. J.J.M.Rowe

Designed by the R & B Partnership
Illustrator: David Anstey
Photography: Peter Millard

Additional photographs:
ZEFA 25, 30 (bottom);
Bruce Iverson/Science Photo Library 19;
Sinclair Stammers/Science Photo Library 30 (top);
Pacific Press Service/Science Photo Library 31 (top).

Dewey Decimal Classification 531
A CIP catalogue record for this book is
available from the British Library

ISBN 0 7496 5623 9

Printed in Malasyia

ACTIVE SCIENCE

Amazing Magnets

Julian Rowe
and Molly Perham

W

FRANKLIN WATTS
LONDON•SYDNEY

Contents

 SAFETY WARNING

Activities marked with this symbol require the presence and help of an adult.

Is it magnetic?

Collect some small objects made of different materials. Hold a magnet over each object, one at a time.

Some of the objects stick to the magnet.

A magnet will pull towards it, or attract, things made of iron. Iron is a magnetic material. Some other metals are also magnetic.

Other things do not stick to the magnet.

Pulling power

Hold a magnet close to a refrigerator door.
Can you feel it being pulled towards the door?
When you let go, the magnet sticks to the door.

The refrigerator door is made
of steel, which contains iron.

Pulling test Find some different magnets, a ruler and a pin.

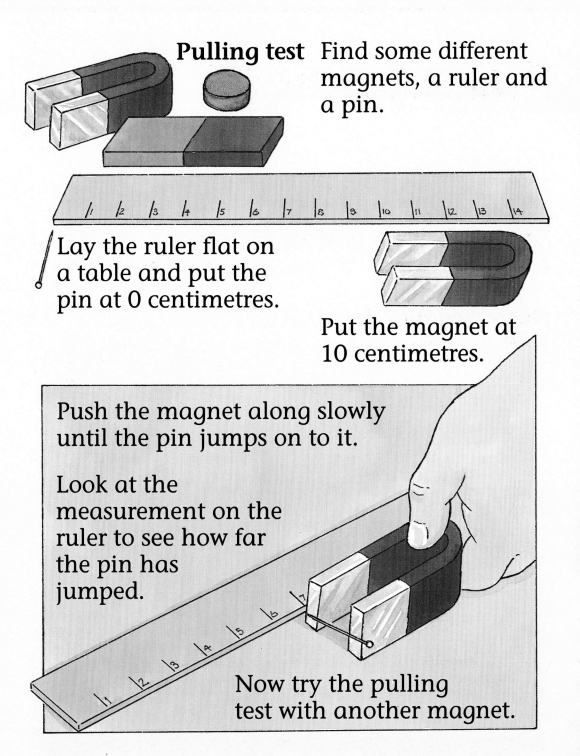

Lay the ruler flat on a table and put the pin at 0 centimetres.

Put the magnet at 10 centimetres.

Push the magnet along slowly until the pin jumps on to it.

Look at the measurement on the ruler to see how far the pin has jumped.

Now try the pulling test with another magnet.

Which one attracts the pin from further away?

More and more magnets

Some magnets are stronger than others.
This magnet easily picks up steel paperclips
from the table. Some of the paperclips are
sticking to each other.

This strong magnet can pick up several spoons.

See how each spoon has become magnetized. It behaves like a magnet and can attract other spoons.

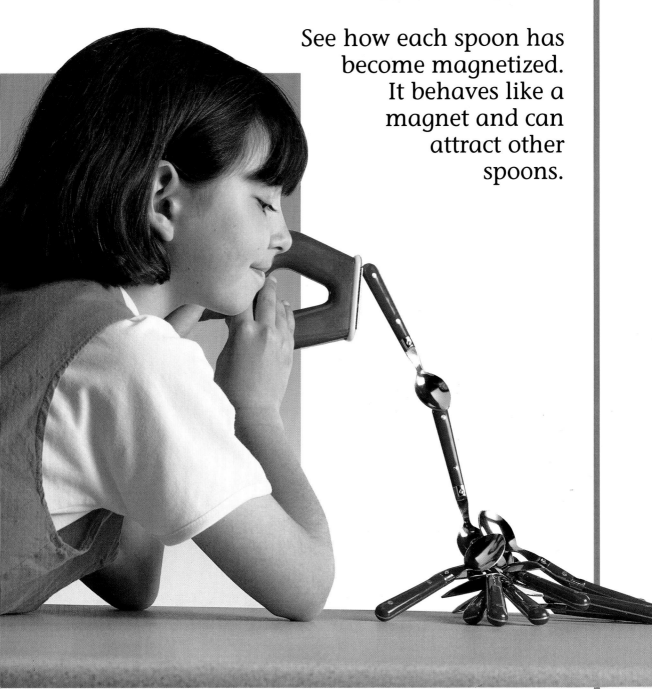

Magnetic games

Have you ever played with a magnetic game? These boys are playing with magnetic counters.

The counters stick to the board. Even if the boys tip the board, the counters do not fall off.

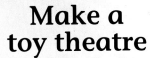

Make a toy theatre

Find a small round magnet, a ruler, sticky tape, a shoe box, some corks, drawing pins, scissors, cardboard and crayons.

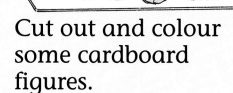

Cut out and colour some cardboard figures.
Ask an adult to make a slit in the top of each cork.
Push the cardboard figures into the slits.

Push a drawing pin into the bottom of each cork.

Tape the magnet to the ruler.

Slide the magnet around under the shoe box to make the figures move.

13

Magnets underwater

Magnets can attract magnetic materials
through water.

Find a magnet, corks, drawing pins, pins, sticky tape, coloured paper, scissors and a plastic bowl.

Push a drawing pin into each cork. Cut out some paper sails. Fix them on with pins and sticky tape.

Fill the bowl with water and put in your cork boats. Hold the magnet underwater.

Can you move the boats around without touching them?

Useful magnets

A magnet also attracts through glass. One part of this magnetic window cleaner is outside the window and the other part is inside. The two parts are held together by a strong magnet.

Many of the things that we use every day have magnets inside them.

A cassette player and its earphones both contain magnets.

The tape you play in your cassette player has a pattern of tiny magnets on it. When the tape is played the cassette player changes the magnetic pattern into sound.

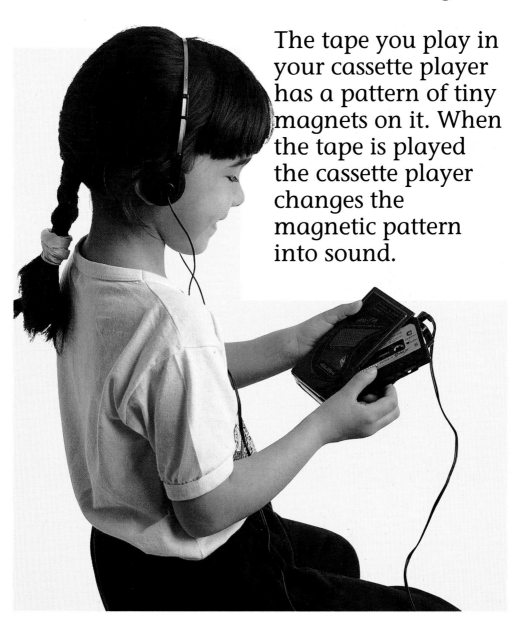

Magnetic field

A magnet's pull, or
force, works in the
space all around it.
This space is called
a magnetic field.
Every magnet
has two places
where the force
is strongest.

You can find out where these are by putting
a magnet into a heap of small panel pins.
Lift the magnet out carefully and see
where most of the pins are sticking.

You cannot see a magnetic field. But you can find out where it is by using tiny pieces of iron called iron filings.

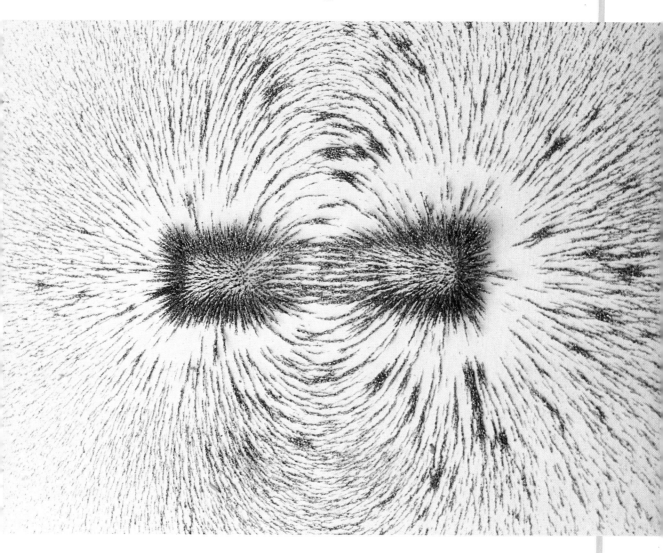

In this picture filings have been sprinkled over a sheet of paper on top of a bar magnet. They clump together where the magnetic field is strongest.

Compasses

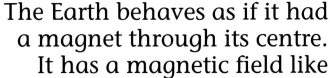

The Earth behaves as if it had a magnet through its centre. It has a magnetic field like other magnets, and north and south poles.

These children are using a compass to find out which direction they are going in.

The needle inside the compass is a magnet. One end always points to the Earth's magnetic north pole.

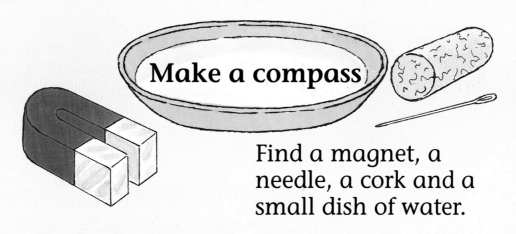

Make a compass

Find a magnet, a needle, a cork and a small dish of water.

Hold the needle steady.
Stroke it with the magnet from one
end to the other, always in the same direction.

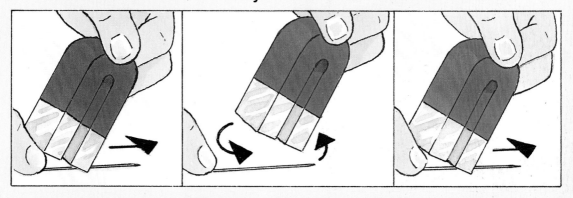

Lift the magnet away from the needle between each stroke.

Ask an adult to cut a slit in the cork. Lay the needle in the slit.

Float the cork in the water. How do you check that your needle points north and south?

21

North and south

The pull of a magnet is strongest at two points called north and south poles. A bar magnet has a pole at each end.

A north pole and a south pole attract each other.

Two south poles push each other apart, or repel each other.

What do you think happens when two north poles are near each other?

Finding north and south

Find a bar magnet, thread, blue and red sticky tape and a compass.

Tie the thread round the middle of the magnet.

Hang the magnet from a hook.

Put blue sticky tape on the end that points south.

Put red sticky tape on the end that points north.

Electromagnets

When electricity flows through a wire it makes a magnetic field around the wire. If you wrap the wire around an iron nail, the nail becomes a strong magnet. This kind of magnet, called an electromagnet, can be turned on and off.

If this boy takes a wire off the battery, the electricity will stop flowing and the paperclips will fall.

This crane has a powerful electromagnet attached to it. When the electricity is switched on, the electromagnet can pick up the heavy scrap iron. When it is switched off, the iron falls down.

In the home

Electromagnets are used in many ways in the home. A telephone has an electromagnet inside.

When someone speaks to you on the phone, electricity flows through the electromagnet inside it. This moves a thin piece of metal up and down.

The movement makes the sounds that we hear.

An electric doorbell uses an electromagnet. When someone presses the bell, electricity flows through the electromagnet inside. This makes a hammer hit against a metal chime.

Motors and magnets

Electric motors have magnets inside them. This toy car has an electric motor that is driven by a battery.

Many machines in your home work with electric motors.

The motor in a vacuum cleaner has electromagnets inside that spin round when the electricity is switched on.

Electric drills and food processors also have electric motors.

Think about... magnets

The first magnets were pieces of lodestone. Before compasses were invented, lodestones were used to find the way.

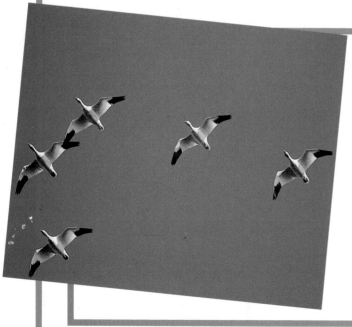

Scientists think that the Earth's magnetic field helps birds to find their way over long distances.

The maglev train has no wheels. It floats above the track. Magnets in the train and in the track repel each other.

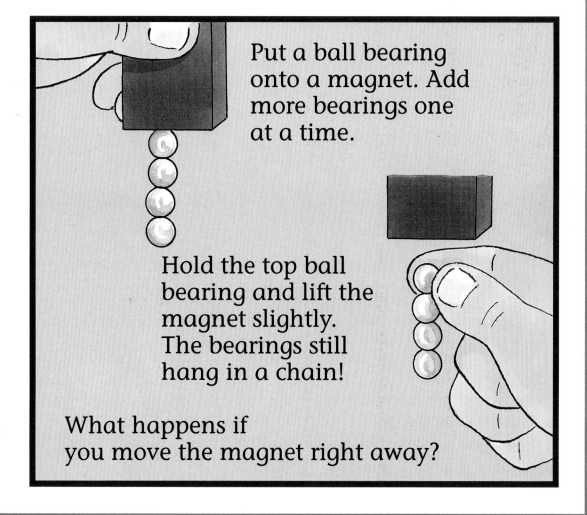

Put a ball bearing onto a magnet. Add more bearings one at a time.

Hold the top ball bearing and lift the magnet slightly. The bearings still hang in a chain!

What happens if you move the magnet right away?